Clayton's River Adventure Continues:
Cincinnati to Frankfort

———— by ————

Linda M. Penn & Frank J. Feger

Illustrated by Matt Adams

Printed in the United States of America

First Printing, 2015

ISBN 978-0-9852488-4-0

Racing to Joy Press
P.O. Box 654
Crestwood, KY 40031

www.LindaMPenn.com/Racing-To-Joy-Press.html

Acknowledgements

To our families and friends for their encouragement and support.

To Marie, Editor, and Matt, Illustrator, for their dedication
and teamwork in this project.

To God for leading our research, and giving us the thoughts
and words for this project.

We are grateful for Panera Bread, Oxmoor Center, providing us the booth
space each week to write another chapter. Amazing how the coffee in the
morning and then those turkey sandwiches at lunchtime provided us the
energy to keep going!

To all the children who will read this book – Happy Reading!

Sincerely,
Frank and Linda

Table of Contents

CHAPTER 1
Sunrise in Cincy

CHAPTER 2
Knowledge and Persuasion

CHAPTER 3
The Purple People Bridge

CHAPTER 4
Books, Books, BOOKS!

CHAPTER 5
This isn't a Cheeseburger!

CHAPTER 6
Sharks ALL Around

CHAPTER 7
WOOOOOOOO!
WOOOOOOOO!
WOOOOOOOO!

CHAPTER 8
The Hero Ship

CHAPTER 9
Clayton's Treasure Chest

CHAPTER 10
Let's go to Carrollton

CHAPTER 11
The Runaway Houseboat

CHAPTER 12
Merging of the Rivers

CHAPTER 13
Twisting, Turning and
Meandering Along

CHAPTER 14
Around the Bend to
Frankfort

CHAPTER 15
A Sweet Surprise

Chapter 1
Sunrise in Cincy

"Rise and shine, get on your sneakers, you adventure seekers, we're going to church service. It is Sunday, remember, and then on a walking tour!" Grampy called to his grandson, Clayton, and his friend, Austin, who were still snug in their sleeping quarters below deck of the Granny Rose.

"Clayton, your mom and I have breakfast ready and we have your assignments. Do you and Austin choose to accept your assignments?" Grampy asked.

"Oh, Grampy, this isn't homework is it, like you gave us before we started this Ohio River cruise?" Clayton responded with a dazed look on his face.

Austin woke up immediately with a bright, happy look on his face. "I'm ready, Grampy! Where are we going?"

At breakfast, Mom grinned as she said, "Hey, guys, we are only a few blocks from St. Peter in Chains Cathedral, where we will go to the church service plus it is very close to the tourist center of the Newport, KY and Cincinnati, Ohio area. Your assignment is to use our Ipad and find out about the history of this cathedral and the Cincinnati / Newport area. Then, the next task is to search about the places we could visit today. We don't want to miss our opportunity for more adventuring, right? Clayton, remember yesterday at your birthday party, you told your dad and Austin's family, 'THE RIVER ADVENTURE CONTINUES!'"

"YES, YES, LET'S DO THIS THING!" the boys responded with pumped fists.

While Mom and the boys cleaned the kitchen and cabin areas, Grampy gathered more supplies at the marina store. Clayton and Austin then reached for the Ipad and began their research. They logged their notes in their journals.

"Man, look at this – an aquarium in Newport! Plus, there is a walking bridge over the Ohio River between Cincinnati and Newport," Clayton said.

"YES!" Austin agreed. "Wait, Clayton, I just thought of something! Let's make up an assignment for Grampy and your mom. We can give them an assignment like they did for us before we left on our Ohio River adventure. Get a clean piece of paper."

"Cool idea!" Clayton answered as he got paper and pen. The boys started their list:

THINGS TO SEE AT THE NEWPORT AQUARIUM

- [ ] Stingrays
- [ ] Hammerhead sharks
- [ ] Scalloped hammerhead sharks
- [ ] Penguins
- [ ] White Alligator
- [ ] Jellyfish
- [ ] Bridge over a shark tank
- [ ] Otters
- [ ] Lizards
- [ ] Different species of fish
- [ ] Turtles

"Let's see if we can research about more to do today in this Newport and Cincy area. You remember last night at the restaurant, we saw all those people with comic books?

There might be a Comic Book Show in town!" Clayton said.

"Wow, look at this," Austin responded. "Comic Book Expo at the Newport Convention Center Saturday and Sunday from 10:00 a.m. to 6:00 p.m."

"We're in! Today is Sunday," Clayton said. "We just have to convince Grampy and Mom to take us to see comic books. Maybe we could even get some autographs and pictures with the writers and illustrators and people all dressed up as comic book characters."

"Got it!" Austin replied. "You know how impressed they were yesterday when we told them all those facts we learned about Louisville and the Ohio River? Let's research the history of the Cincy area and the St. Peter in Chains Cathedral right now. When we impress them with all of our new knowledge, surely they won't refuse when we beg them to take us to the Comic Book Show."

"We're on it, man!" Clayton exclaimed.

Chapter 2
Knowledge and Persuasion

"Mom, Grampy, guess what we learned," Clayton boasted as Grampy returned with the supplies.

As Clayton and Austin closed the Ipad and reviewed their journal notes, they couldn't wait to share their new knowledge.

"The St. Peter in Chains Cathedral was started in 1841 and finished in 1845," Austin began spewing his knowledge.

"Four years! A long time to build," Clayton added. "Gosh, how huge is this place?"

"It probably took a long time to build because churches here in America were built modeled after the gigantic cathedrals in Europe. They were very tall and had a steeple," Grampy answered.

"Let's start our walk, guys," Mom said. "We can head toward the church and go to Mass there. On the way, you can continue to share all that new knowledge about this area."

Clayton nudged Austin and they nodded to each other, believing their plan to impress with knowledge was working.

"We uncovered this about the Cincinnati history, "Clayton said. "The city was founded in 1788 by people from Germany who traveled down the Ohio River from the East. The Ohio was the main route to the West."

"Seems weird to say Cincinnati was the West," Austin said.

"Yes, but the western United States of today wasn't even explored yet. Lewis and Clark didn't begin their Western Expedition until 1804," Grampy recalled.

"Guess what else we learned about Cincinnati?" Austin volunteered. The city grew in population because many Revolutionary War soldiers settled around here after the Northwest Territory Governor named Arthur St. Clair began honoring returning soldiers."

"And the city grew just like in Louisville, because of the steamboat traffic bringing jobs," Clayton added.

Grampy and Mom looked proudly at the boys. "High Five!" Grampy said, as he and Mom clapped hands with them.

"Oh, wow, look how pretty the church is," Mom said as they approached St. Peter in Chains Cathedral. She touched the stone wall with reverence. "How tall the steeple is! No wonder it took four years to build this place," she continued.

As everyone looked upward at the height of the steeple, Austin shouted, "I'm getting dizzy! First, you guys made me have claustrophobia about a concrete box and the locks on the Ohio yesterday. Now you are making me dizzy today looking at this steeple! Can we just go on inside to Mass now? I wonder how tall the ceiling is?"

"Okay, man, let's do this," Clayton said as he pushed Austin through the church door. "Just don't look up. Stay low, buddy!"

After church service, as they were continuing their walk around town toward the walking bridge over the Ohio to Newport, KY, Grampy asked," What else did you guys learn about Cincinnati, Newport, and what is happening around here today?"

Clayton and Austin gazed at each other and knew this was the time to try some persuasion to get to that Comic Show.

"Well...since you asked," Clayton said shyly.

Chapter 3
The Purple People Bridge

"Okay, let's have it!" Mom opened her arms with anticipation and smiled. "Let's start our walking tour over the Purple People Bridge between Cincy and Newport. Grampy and I are all ears. Tell us the itinerary. By the way, don't get so excited that you run into other walkers or bicyclists."

"Got it!" Clayton answered. "Austin and I investigated about the Newport Aquarium. We're sure you would like going there, and we even have an assignment for you and Grampy."

"If you choose to accept this assignment, of course." Austin tried to maintain a serious face.

"Are you trying to imitate me?" Grampy laughed.

Clayton reached in his pocket and pulled out

Clayton and Austin's List of Things to See at the Newport Aquarium. "Just for you, Mom and Grampy."

Austin and Clayton shared a high five.

"Okay, okay, we agree," Mom and Grampy shook the boys' hands.

"There is something else..."Austin stammered. "There is a Comic Book Expo at the Newport Convention Center." Austin's head bent down to his chest. He stopped in his tracks and closed his eyes - a scene of embarrassment.

"Really? That's AWESOME!" Grampy beamed. I still have some comic books stored away."

"So do I," Mom grinned.

"You do?" Clayton and Austin looked at the adults in total amazement. "You mean you read comic books?"

"YES!" Grampy and Mom responded.

"Hey, guys, we aren't that old!" Mom just shook her head.

"The Convention Center is on the way to the Newport Aquarium." Grampy pointed the way. "You can probably get some pictures with the authors and illustrators."

"Cool! And autographs! Come on, let's go, Grampy and Mom." Clayton motioned for everyone to hurry.

"Hey you two, we'll get there, hold on, I see the Belle of Cincinnati. Let's look closer," Mom said as she moved over to the railing and peered down at the big boat traveling out from under the bridge.

"That boat is A-OK," Clayton said, as he bent over the railing. "It's huge."

Just then, Clayton backed away from the railing and looked straight ahead.

"What's up, man?" Austin asked as he saw Clayton's glassy-eyed expression.

"You look sick!"

"I'll be fine, as long as I stay in the middle of this bridge. No looking down for me."

"Hey, that's okay! I got dizziness from looking straight up at the cathedral steeple. Plus, I had claustrophia in the Ohio River locks. So you get queasy from looking way down over the railing of the Purple People Bridge? Now we're even!" Austin said as he clapped his hands and did a thumbs up for Clayton.

"Okay, Austin, come over here and look how the Belle of Cincinnati looks different from our Belle of Louisville," Grampy said. "That paddlewheel on the Cincinnati boat is so much smaller that the Louisville paddlewheel. The Cincinnati boat has a different way of propelling itself through the water. Her paddlewheel is just a decoration."

"Grampy, I volunteer to do research on the

differences between the boats before we come back to the Cincy area this summer." Austin eagerly said, but then he stopped, getting red-faced. "Well...I mean...if we come back here...well I mean... if you ask me to come back with you," Austin said quietly.

"Can't do a river adventure without you, deckhand!" Grampy knuckle-bumped Austin.

"Look at all those bridges over the Ohio," Clayton yelled from the middle of the bridge. "We don't have that many bridges in Louisville."

"You're right, Cincy has a total of nine bridges," Mom added.

"So many hills, too!" Austin pointed to the Cincinnati skyline, as they neared the end of the bridge to Newport.

"Cincy has seven hills," Grampy answered.

Oh, just like the seven hills of Rome," Clayton boasted. "Aren't you proud of me? I remember that from history class."

"Enough!" Austin threw up his hands. "The comic books are calling us!"

"Yes, look at those people over there, all dressed up in their costumes ready to go to the Expo," Grampy agreed as they exited the bridge.

"Follow the Darth Vader character!" Clayton

requested.

"Yes, and the Wonder Woman character!" Mom said with excitement.

"THE ADVENTURE CONTINUES!" Clayton called motioning everyone toward the Expo Center.

Chapter 4
Books, Books, BOOKS!

"Grampy, look at all these people dressed as comic book and movie characters! All these tables full of comic books and DVD's," Clayton said.

"Welcome to Comic Book Expo!" said a Superman character. "Here is your Comic Con Program listing everyone here - the characters, artists, and writers along with their table numbers."

"Thank you!" Mom shook the hand of the tall, muscle-bound Superman. "May we have a picture with you?"

"Sure, everyone here at the Expo loves having pictures taken." The Superman character smiled as he put his arms around Mom and the boys while Grampy took the picture.

"What a wingspan that guy had!" Austin declared as he, Clayton, Mom and Grampy proceeded through the turnstile. "We should have asked him if he played basketball anywhere!"

The boys could see the rows and rows of tables, each with a tall pole showing a number. People were milling about snapping pictures with the artists and getting their autographs.

"Look at this list!" Clayton marveled. "So many choices of people to see. Hey, Mom, Grampy, could we..." Clayton's voice trailed off as he lowered his head.

"The answer is yes," Mom laughed. "You don't have to be embarrassed to ask about buying some comic books today."

"Now, just how did you know what I was thinking?" Clayton shook his head.

"Moms know everything, right" Grampy grinned.

"Okay, okay, let's get started." Clayton pointed to the Program. "To the Green Lantern, Table Number 10! And look, the Loop and Hoodie artist, Dan Cassity, is here! Table 12."

Austin peered over Clayton's shoulder. "Is Spiderman on there?"

"Right here, Table Number 18!" Clayton answered.

"I want to visit the G. I. Joe table," Grampy said. "Maybe I can find some toys for my collection. Did you youngsters know I was in Germany as a G. I. Joe, for real, back in the 1960's? Your Granny Rose was with me. We lived in Frankfurt, Germany for two years. I was very proud to be in the U. S. Army.

"Good for you, Grampy!" Austin and Clayton said, giving salutes to Grampy.

"Here's the G. I. Joe Table." Clayton pointed to the Comic Con Program. "It's Table Number 9, right next to my Green Lantern Table."

"My turn now?" Mom raised her hand and waved.

As she searched the listings, her eyes grew wide. "Star Wars, Tables 20 and 21. Wow, two tables! Maybe all the characters are there – Skywalker, Darth Vader, CP30, R2D2, and my favorite, Princess Leah."

"I have an idea. Let's split up," Grampy said. "Austin and Mom, you go together since your tables are close to each other. Clayton and I will go together. We'll meet at the exit door in 30 minutes. Are you hungry yet? It's lunch time for me! Let's go to the Hofbrauhaus. We passed it on the way here. It's a German restaurant."

"Wait, I don't know any German words. The only German food I have ever heard of is wiener schnitzel.

I remember Mom and Dad talking about it one time."
Austin looked bewildered.

"Trust me, it will be okay," Grampy said, grinning, and then he and Mom started laughing. He gave Austin a pat on the back.

Clayton and Austin looked at each other and shrugged their shoulders as they began their Comic Book Expo journey.

"Something's up, your mom and Grampy are acting weird again," Austin said.

"Oh, yeah!" Clayton confirmed. "See you in 30."

Chapter 5
This isn't a Cheeseburger!

"Grampy, this German restaurant will have cheeseburgers on the menu, right?" Clayton asked, as the group headed from the Comic Book Expo to Hofbrauhaus. Clayton and Austin both had bewildered looks.

"Oh, yeah!" Grampy agreed, nodding his head. His eyes were sparkling, but had that gleam of deception in them.

"Clayton, your Grampy...do you think..." Austin's voice trailed off as he elbowed Clayton. "Do you think he is trying to trick us about the cheeseburgers at this restaurant?"

"Grampy, what's up?" Clayton asked.

"What do you mean, fellows? I promise, scouts honor, that they have cheeseburgers," Grampy said in a strong voice, while Mom gave two thumbs up.

"And since I thought we would be coming to Hofbrauhas on our Ohio River trip," Grampy continued, "I brought along this German American reference book." Grampy pulled a dog-eared, well-worn, little book from his back pocket. "Your Granny Rose and I used this all the time when we lived in Germany years ago. I'm glad I kept it. You guys might like to scan through it before we eat."

"Hey, fellows, here we are," Mom announced as they walked to the restaurant door. "I can't wait to eat some weisswurst and sauerkraut."

Clayton grimaced. "As long as they have cheeseburgers, I will be good."

As the group sat in the lobby, Grampy returned from the receptionist's desk. "20 minutes for a table, you adventurers! You want to look through the German reference book while we wait?"

"Sure thing," Austin said. "I want to search for 'wiener schnitzel.' My parents said they really liked it. I wonder if it is just a fancy name for hot dog and pretzels?"

After handing the book to the boys, Grampy and Mom surveyed the memorabilia and souvenirs in the glass cases in the lobby. They found steins with Bavarian Alps scenes and lids.

"Why do steins have lids?" Mom asked Grampy.

"To keep the flies out of your drink in the summertime. A lot of dining in Germany is outdoors in the warm seasons."

"I might buy one of these on our way out." Mom pretended to be taking a drink from a stein.

"Did you see the Black Forest cuckoo clocks? Made from real Black Forest wood. You might change your mind and get one of these instead of a stein." Grampy laughed.

"Yes, they are beautiful. I love the one with the rabbits, birds, and reindeer going around in the circle." Mom said.

Just then, a beautiful blue bird popped out of the clock and cuckooed the hour of 12:00 noon. "Pretty, but not sure I can take the cuckoo noise! Think I will stick with the stein." Mom laughed as she covered her ears.

Back in the waiting area, Austin and Clayton were engrossed in Grampy's German American reference book. Austin showed Clayton a picture of 'wiener schnitzel' and read that it was made of beef, covered in flour, beaten egg, and breadcrumbs, then fried.

"Hmm...maybe I'll order this instead of a cheeseburger," Austin said rubbing his stomach.

"Not me," Clayton answered. "Cheeseburger all the way. Let's see if we can find what Mom wants. What was it...weisswurst?"

"Got it, look here." Austin pointed to the picture and definition in Grampy's book. "It is white sausage. Hey, I like sausage, but WHITE sausage?" Austin turned up his nose. "Well, if your Mom likes it, that's super, but I'm sticking to the wiener schnitzel."

"Our table is ready!" Grampy called to the boys as the restaurant pager buzzed.

"Grampy, what are you going to order, and can we get an appetizer of bretzels and cheese? Clayton asked as the group scanned the menu.

"Sure," Grampy and Mom answered together.

"I am eager to enjoy some pretzels." Mom pointed to the picture on the menu.

"Mom, we learned it is BRETZELS, with a B. See what we learned from your book, Grampy?" Clayton and Austin looked at Mom and Grampy with proud faces.

"Good job, guys!" Mom laughed. "Here comes our waitress, and we will definitely order Bretzels...with a B. What a pretty German dirndl dress she is wearing."

"I will have a Munchner bratwurst with red cabbage," Grampy told the waitress after Mom and the boys ordered.

"RED CABBAGE?" the boys said together. They both squinted their eyes shut and shook their heads.

"Wow, white sausage, red cabbage, this restaurant is definitely colorful!" Austin said.

After eating their appetizer, the waitress carried their meals to the table. Everyone marveled at how delicious the food looked, except Clayton. He just sat there and stared at his plate. He looked up, opened his mouth to talk, and then glanced down at his food again.

Trying to maintain his composure, Clayton sat up straight and blushed as he said, "Grampy, this isn't a cheeseburger. Where is the top? Will you call the waitress back and ask her about the top for the bun?"

Grampy had that tricky look in his eyes again. "It's an open-faced cheeseburger. You have to use your die gabel and das messer to eat it."

"Oh, Grampy, you knew that all along, didn't you, when you said this place had cheeseburgers, tricky, tricky!" Clayton shook his finger at Grampy.

Everyone laughed, including Clayton.

"Okay, let's say grace and dig in!" Grampy suggested.

"I am going to save room for some apfel strudel before we head to the Newport Aquarium," Mom rubbed her hands together in anticipation.

"Yes, we need to get back to the Ohio River adventure!" Grampy declared.

Chapter 6
Sharks ALL around

Hey, you young adventurers, there is a new exhibit here at the Newport Aquarium called Shark Bridge." Grampy showed them a poster in the lobby of the aquarium.

"Could we go to the Shark Bridge first?" Clayton looked at the layout of the aquatic exhibits on the aquarium brochure. "Wow, it is a V-shaped rope suspension bridge and it is 75 feet long."

"Sounds good to me," Grampy said.

"Don't forget your list, "Things to See at the Newport Aquarium." Austin handed the list to Grampy.

"Are you sure we will be able to cross off all these things in one day?" Mom commented as she peered over Grampy's shoulder at the list.

"We will see as much as we can. Of course, we need to break anchor from the marina slip by 4:30 this afternoon or else we will have to pay for another day. The Granny Rose is 42 feet long and the charge is $2.00 a foot per day.

"That's $84.00!" Austin calculated. "We need to roll!"

"Okay, I have been studying this map, follow me! To the Shark Bridge!" Clayton motioned straight ahead.

As the group found the Shark Bridge exhibit, they saw a platform with ropes on each side just inches above a huge circular tank filled with sharks.

"Wait, you sharkanados, read this sign. It lists all the types of sharks in this tank."

Grampy said. "There are seven different species of sharks in there and there are 385,000 gallons of water."

"I am going to write these names down in my journal. Could I use the Ipad and research about them later? Then when I call my Mom and Dad tonight, I can tell them all about these sharks," Austin said as he jotted down notes.

"Absolutely," Grampy said. "Glad to see you are so interested in learning. When we get back on the river, you will have time to gain some more intriguing information about these fish."

"Hey, Mom, are you okay?" Clayton noticed his mother sweating a little and looking strange. "Scared?" he asked her.

"Well...sorta...maybe...well...YES... I'll just meet you fellows on the other side by the shark tunnel." Mom wiped her forehead. "Not sure about these sharks all around my feet." She tip-toed backward from the bridge entrance and headed toward a drinking fountain. "You have fun, okay?"

"Yes, we promise we won't be lunch for the sharks." Grampy smiled as he gave the boys a gentle shove by the 'Please stay in a single file line when crossing this bridge' sign.

As the group walked tentatively across the bridge, they gained confidence in the sturdiness of the bridge and the boys started skipping. Grampy continued his slow, careful steps.

"Grampy, you weren't scared, were you?" Clayton asked when they exited the bridge. "You were...hmm, how should I say this? Well, you were pretty slow bringing up the rear."

"Scared? Well...no...not exactly...just wanted to be sure-footed." It was Grampy's turn to head for the drinking fountain.

"Mom, that was the absolute COOLEST!" Clayton exclaimed as he and Austin ran up to her. They hummed the song from the movie about sharks.

"So glad you had fun with the sharks all around," Mom said, looking relieved to see everyone made the crossing safely.

"Definitely exciting," Grampy said, shaking his head "Now, where is our list of things to see?"

Mom and Grampy crossed off the animals on their list they had seen so far.

"I have an idea. Clayton wanted to see the sharks, which we just did. The rest of us could each pick an exhibit," Grampy urged as he checked his watch.

"Good idea, I would like to see the penguins," Mom said.

"Great, could I please see the alligators?" Austin asked.

"Good choices, and I would like to see the tropical fish." Grampy requested. "Clayton, you have the map. Chart our course for us."

"I'm on it!" Clayton said as he unfolded the map.

"Then it is back to the Granny Rose?" asked Austin.

"Yes, casting off within the next hour and a half." Grampy looked at his watch again. "Then it's back to the Ohio River!"

Chapter 7
WOOOOOOOO! WOOOOOOOO! WOOOOOOOO!

"Clayton and Austin, I have the Departure Checklist here," Grampy said as the group boarded the Granny Rose after their aquarium adventure.

"Man, the aquarium was AWESOME, so was the Comic Expo! I don't know which place I liked the best. Too bad we didn't get to see all the marine exhibits. I will be sorry to leave Cincinnati and Newport," Clayton lamented.

"Me too!" Austin agreed. "I know what my favorite place was – the German restaurant!

"Oh, come on, I had to eat my cheeseburger with a knife and fork – no bun!" Clayton complained.

"My favorite place was the restaurant too," Mom said

as she stored the box with her new Black Forest cuckoo clock in the bedroom.

"Sure hope that bluebird doesn't wake us up at night, Mom. CUCKOO, CUCKOO, CUCKOO," Clayton mimicked the bird.

"We'll be fine, I will use it as a beautiful decoration in the hallway, rather than having it make noise. I will not reset the weights. Then it will not go CUCKOO! Can't wait to tell your dad about it when we call him tonight."

"Yes, speaking of stopping for the night, we will never get underway and get back down the Ohio unless we go through this checklist and shove off," Grampy coaxed.

"Okay," Austin said. "Give us our assignments. I am ready to roll."

"Number 1 – Water tank gauge. Does it say 'full?' If not, we will have to top it off before we disconnect from the marina outlet."

"Check, water gauge reads 'full.' Austin made a checkmark on Grampy's list.

"Numbers 2 and 3 are for me," Grampy declared. "Fuel tanks are full. We have 300 gallons, plenty to get to Carrollton, and our batteries are A-OK."

"What's next, Grampy?" Clayton asked.

"Number 4 - Run light and navigation lights,"

Grampy answered. "I will turn on all the lights and you guys can check to see if the red and green navigation lights in the forward section are working. Then, check the aft section for the white run light. We need these lights to tell other boaters where we are and which direction we are headed. The red light is on the right or starboard side and the green light is on the left or port side."

"Check, all lights in order." Clayton reported.

"Number 5 – Pumps. I pumped out the gray water tank already at the marina, so the sewage is gone, and I have disconnected our pump from the marina storage facility. We never want to dump our sewage straight into the river. We want to keep our river as clean as possible, right?"

"Sure thing!" Clayton agreed.

"Now what is our next job, Grampy?" Austin asked.

"Number 6 – Bumpers and Ropes. Will you deckhands help Mom store the bumpers and ropes?"

"Check, bumpers and ropes stored." Mom checked off the last thing on Grampy's list.

"All right! Anchors away!" Grampy motioned to the south as he started the engine of the Granny Rose and backed out of the marina slip.

"Okay, Grampy, we are off to our look-out post on the

top deck. We will warn you about any large debris or logs."
Clayton gave Grampy a salute.

After a couple of hours of watching out and reading
their new comic books, Clayton and Austin climbed down
the ladder to the main cabin and began rubbing their
stomachs.

"Yes, I get the hint. Clayton, how about coming down
to the galley and helping me?" Mom said. "Sandwiches
and chips coming up. Plus, we still have some cake and ice
cream. While we are fixing dinner, Austin and Grampy, will
you be on the lookout for a small creek draining into the
Ohio? I read an article recently about an abandoned vessel
in a creek off the Ohio about 25 miles south of Cincy across
from Lawrenceburg, Indiana."

"I remember that too," Grampy commented. "We
have traveled about 25 miles and we are approaching
Lawrenceburg, Indiana according to the river map."

WOOOOOOOO! WOOOOOOOO! WOOOOOOOO!

Mom, Grampy, Clayton, and Austin stood frozen.

"I noticed the wind was getting up. Now, it is blowing
harder," Austin said as he shivered.

WOOOOOOOOOOOOO! WOOOOOOO!
WOOOOOOOOO!

"It's getting darker, is it going to rain and storm?"

Clayton asked as he shivered too.

"Maybe a few showers, but no storms predicted tonight," Mom noted after checking the weather app on her phone.

"Grampy, then, just what was that noise? Was it another boat whistle? I don't see any other boats close by." Clayton moved closer to Grampy.

"Let's use the spotlight," Mom suggested, as she and Austin also moved closer to Grampy.

Grampy took the spotlight control stick on the dashboard in the wheelhouse and aimed it down the creek. There was a huge boat sitting in the creek about 100 yards down from the Ohio. It looked like two big green eyes were peering out from the newly found boat.

Clayton and Austin screamed and covered their eyes.

"Guys, this is fantastic," Mom exclaimed. "I think we have found the ghost ship in this creek!"

The boys screamed again. "GHOST SHIP?"

"That noise was the wind blowing through the whistle stacks on the ship," Grampy commented. "We can drop anchor here at the mouth of this creek for the night. We will be able to explore in the morning," Grampy said. "I will need to check the depth gauge on the Granny Rose. She needs at least three feet of water to navigate the creek up to the ghost ship.

"You mean we are going to explore the GHOST SHIP?" Clayton shook again.

Chapter 8
The Hero Ship

After securing anchors at the forward and aft parts of the Granny Rose and shutting down the engine, Grampy checked the generator to make sure it was operating properly. "Check, electricity maintained," he said.

"Food's ready, come and get it," Mom called.

"We are on it!" Austin said as he and Grampy moved to the galley.

The evening lights from Lawrenceburg, Indiana across the river were on and the moon and clouds were appearing as the group ate dinner on the top deck.

"Hey, look at that moon and the clouds," Clayton pointed to the skies over the Ohio. "Do you see what I see? Those clouds are forming the outline of a ghost over the moon."

"Oh, come on, get real, buddy!" Austin patted Clayton on the shoulder. "Grampy, may Clayton and I use the Ipad to search about an abandoned ship in a creek in Kentucky?

"Sure, good idea." Grampy handed the boys the Ipad. "You will sleep better tonight if you know a little more about the history of this vessel and that there are really NO ghosts onboard."

"Don't stay up all night searching on the Ipad, you adventurers. It's been a full day," Mom cautioned.

"Let's make our phone calls to our families back home and then we need to get to bed. We want an early start in the morning - as soon as the sun comes up!" Grampy laughed.

After the phone calls, the boys went below to the lower bunk.

"Lights out in 15 minutes!" Grampy called down.

"Austin, look at this!" Clayton showed the Ipad to Austin. "This boat was launched in 1902! Man, that is OLD! It has gone through several names over the years. These pictures show how rusty and dilapidated the boat is now."

"This boat went through World War I and World War II." Austin showed Clayton the paragraph about how it helped to patrol waterways around Key West, Florida and then Long Island Sound in New York during the wars.

"Wow, Austin, look, check out this part!" Clayton shouted.

"Thomas Edison, THE THOMAS EDISON, as in the famous inventor THOMAS EDISON, experimented on the boat. The U.S. Navy asked him to do research about ways to detect any submarines."

"So after the wars, it became a sightseeing boat in New York harbor." Austin directed Clayton to the picture of the boat with Circle Line V on it.

"SERIOUSLY! THIS BOAT IS HISTORIC! LIKE, IT IS AWESOME! Does the article say how it ended up in this creek?" Clayton wondered.

"Got it," Austin said. "It says this guy named Robert Miller bought this boat in 1986 in New Jersey, fixed it up, and decided to bring it down here to Northern Kentucky to the land he owned."

"HEY, YOU DECKHANDS," Grampy called downstairs to the boys' bunks, "TIME TO GO TO SLEEP!"

"Okay, we'll try," Clayton switched the Ipad off and turned out the lights, but the night brought restless sleep to the boys.

"Hey, man, are you awake?" Austin whispered to Clayton as the night wore on.

"Sorta," Clayton said as he raised up in his bunk and hit his head on the low ceiling. "Ouch!"

"You know what? I keep dreaming about that ship," Austin proclaimed, seeming to ignore Clayton rubbing his head. "Can you imagine what it would have been like to be onboard and patrol in American waterways during the World Wars? Talk about heroes!"

"They should call that ship 'hero ship,' Clayton said sleepily. "Can I go back to sleep now?"

The next morning, after breakfast, and after more research on the Ipad, everyone was ready to explore. Grampy maneuvered the Granny Rose up the creek. As the sun gleamed through the low-hanging limbs of the trees, the group saw a man wearing a captain's hat standing on the front of the ship.

"Permission to come aboard?" Grampy asked. "May we tie the nose of our houseboat to the nose of your boat?"

"Permission granted," the man hollered back.

As the group stepped onto the abandoned ship, the man shook their hands. "Welcome aboard. My name is Captain Miller."

"Captain MILLER? Your last name is MILLER?" Clayton showed the man their Ipad. "We researched and found out a man named Miller bought this boat and brought it here from New York City. Are you that Mr. Miller?" Clayton said shyly.

"No, that was my father," Captain Miller smiled. "Would you like to explore this vessel?"

"YES!" both boys exclaimed.

"Can't believe this ship was in two wars plus THE THOMAS EDISON was actually on board here. Austin and I think it should be called a HERO SHIP, not a GHOST SHIP," Clayton declared.

"We know some of the ship's history," Mom said. "But can you tell us how it came to be abandoned here?"

"Don't know exactly what Dad was thinking, but I know that he and his crew navigated the ship from New York City, through the Great Lakes, down the Mississippi River, and up the Ohio River. He used the boat as a sightseeing vessel around Cincinnati and then eventually parked it for good here in this creek by the land that he bought."

Captain Miller led the group around the ship, cautioning them to be careful. "Remember this ship is very old – over 100 years! Let's go forward to the wheelhouse area and see where the controls were."

"Oh, there's the green eyes we saw last night with Grampy's spotlight." Austin pointed to the two steam gauges on the back wall of the control room.

Everyone laughed as they followed Captain Miller. "I don't want you to miss the storage room below the sightseeing deck. It's cold, damp, and dark down there, but I have a small flashlight."

"Dark? Cold? Damp? Below deck? Only a small flashlight? What could be down there in the belly of this boat? Is this really a GHOST ship?" Clayton whispered to Austin. They both got the shivers again.

Chapter 9
Clayton's Treasure Chest

Captain Miller, Clayton, and Austin descended the narrow ladder into the bottom of the ship while Grampy and Mom stayed up-top.

"Sure hope you have a fresh set of batteries in your flashlight, Captain Miller," Clayton commented. He rubbed his eyes as he tried to adjust to the dim light.

"We're fine," Captain Miller laughed.

Clayton and Austin elbowed each other and the faint light cast a shadow of doubt over their frozen faces.

"You're su...huh...sure?" Austin's voice quivered.

"Absolutely, guys," Captain Miller said in a trusting manner. "Look over at these shelves."

The boys saw lots of wooden crates and barrels sitting around, along with piles of rusty mechanical and electrical parts.

"I wonder - Did THE THOMAS EDISON use any of this old equipment in his experiments?" Clayton asked.

"It's certainly possible," Captain Miller replied.

"We found articles on the Internet about this ship being called a 'ghost ship' but Clayton and I decided to call it a 'hero ship.' Austin's voice was sounding more confident now.

"Fantastic idea," Captain Miller said. "My dad would be proud of you both."

As Captain Miller and the boys continued examining the storage area, one of the bottom boards popped up close to Clayton's feet revealing what looked to be a small, rusty chest in the opening between the boards.

"Captain Miller, could you shine the flashlight in this opening on the floor?" Clayton asked.

"Okay." Captain Miller shone his light at the opening and the boys could see the surprised and excited look on the captain's face.

"Oh, fellows, look at this chest! I thought I had explored every inch of this boat. I never saw this before. Clayton, can you pull that box through the opening while I hold the loose board aside? We may have found treasure!"

"A TREASURE CHEST?" Clayton and Austin

screamed together.

"Let's take this chest upstairs to the daylight," Captain Miller said as he and Clayton removed it from the opening.

"What's going on down there?" Grampy called with concern in his voice.

"We think we found a TREASURE CHEST!" Clayton yelled.

Back upstairs in the sunlight, the group was trying to open the box. The seal was still intact. Mom jiggled the lock mechanism and it broke completely off.

"Oh, no! Sorry, Captain Miller, I didn't mean to break it." Mom was shaking her head as she kept apologizing.

"No problem," Captain Miller consoled. "We can get into this box more easily now." Captain Miller pried the box open as the seal broke.

"How much money is in there?" Clayton inquired.

"Hey, buddy, I don't see any money, just a bunch of papers, a book, and some maps. Sorry, dude," Austin said.

"Hold on, fellows," Captain Miller said as he handed the contents to Grampy who spread everything out on main deck floor.

Clayton got his journal out from his back pocket and

made a list: Ship Manifest, A History of Travels; Circle V Passenger List; Research Notes, and maps of the Caribbean Sea, New York harbor, Great Lakes, Mississippi River, and the Ohio River.

"Mom, Grampy, Captain Miller, Austin, these research notes are signed by 'T.E.' You know who that means, don't you? None other than THE THOMAS EDISON!" Clayton touched the notes with gentleness and reverence.

"What can we do with these documents?" Mom asked. "They are in remarkably good condition."

"Got it! We could take them to the Kentucky History Center in Frankfort. With your permission of course, Captain Miller," Clayton suggested. "Hey, Austin, remember last year when we went there on a school field trip? The place is so cool, with all those old things."

"Oh, yes!," Austin agreed.

"Grampy, would you like to make a call there to see if they are interested? I certainly give my permission." Captain Miller nodded.

Grampy took the cell phone, found the number, and started making the call to the Kentucky Historical Society at the Thomas D. Clark Center for Kentucky History. The group continued to scan through the documents. They found the passenger lists of the Circle V contained names and address of people all over the world.

"Great news," reported Grampy. "Sara, the Curator, said she would really like to review these documents for a possible exhibit at the History Center."

"Fantastic," Captain Miller declared. "Clayton, would you like to present the papers to the History Center? We wouldn't have found them unless you noticed the chest."

"REALLY?" Clayton shouted. His jaws dropped, his mouth opened wide, and his eyes became as large as silver dollars.

"We could take a detour today on our way home to Louisville," Grampy suggested. We just need to travel south on the Ohio River, turn into the Kentucky River at Carrollton, and proceed through four sets of locks to Frankfort."

"MORE LOCKS? You mean four more concrete boxes?" Austin laughed.

"THE ADVENTURE CONTINUES!" Clayton smiled as he and Austin did their fist bumps.

Chapter 10
Let's go to Carrollton

As Grampy started the engines of the Granny Rose,
Mom and the boys untied the ropes from the ghost ship.
Grampy pulled the gears into reverse and checked the
depth gauge. He maneuvered the boat from the creek
into the Ohio River at mile marker 494 to proceed to
the Markland Dam and Locks, to Carrollton, KY and the
Kentucky River, and then to Frankfort, KY.

"Clayton and Austin," Grampy grabbed the attention
of the boys in an authoritative voice. "Did you know
that I have a famous ancestor – George Rogers Clark?
You remember learning about him when you did your
homework on the history of Louisville, right?"

"Yes," Clayton responded. "There is a statue of him in
downtown Louisville."

"Wasn't Clarksville, Indiana named for him?" Austin asked.

"No, actually it was named for William Clark, George's brother. William established the Clarksville settlement in 1784. Then he and Meriwether Lewis began their famous westward expedition in 1803."

"Wow, what famous ancestors!" Clayton exclaimed. "That makes me sorta like a relative of George Rogers Clark AND William Clark!"

"Yes, next time you see the George Rogers Clark statue, you'll have more to think about," Mom said.

"Is that where I get my adventurous spirit?" Clayton laughed.

"All these famous ancestors, can I find a famous relative too?" Austin pondered.

"The Kentucky History Center has a research library, but I got most of my ancestry information from the Filson Club in Louisville," Grampy commented.

"Sounds like a project for Mom, Dad, and me this summer," Austin grinned.

"How about you young adventurers researching on the Ipad for information on the Kentucky River and Carrollton while we travel down the Ohio?" Mom suggested.

"Will do," Clayton agreed as he and Austin picked up the Ipad and headed to the top deck to assume their lookout posts.

After a couple of hours of relaxing, reading, and waving to other boaters, the boys heard Grampy calling, "Come down fellows, we need to get the ropes and bumpers ready. We are approaching the Markland Locks."

"On it," the boys answered.

"I will call the Lockmaster on the marine radio, channel 13, to determine if we can proceed through the locks now or if we will need to wait for a barge or other boats to complete their locks journey first," Grampy said.

"Check! Bumpers and ropes ready," Mom declared.

"The Lockmaster said we can proceed to tie up on the port side of the locks," Grampy said.

"Concrete box coming up!" Austin yelled as he and Clayton moved the bumpers and ropes to the left side of the Granny Rose.

After completing the locks journey, Austin gave a two thumbs up and boasted, "That was exciting, but not so scary, like yesterday. It is awesome to think how these concrete locks were built, with doors opening and closing to the river water."

"Good observation," Mom said. "Now, let's go to Carrollton! We can anchor there and get lunch." Mom pointed down river.

"Okay, Austin and I know exactly where to eat – the Carrollton Inn or Welch's Riverside Restaurant. Both have good menus and views of the rivers where they come together." Clayton rubbed his stomach as he continued, "Our Ipad research said the Carrollton Inn was a famous restaurant and rooming house for steamboat captains back in the early 1800's. All kinds of items from Eastern Kentucky were brought down the Kentucky River to Carrollton for shipping to Louisville, St. Louis, New Orleans to the south or to Pittsburgh up east.

"We made a list of products that were transported," Austin offered as he proudly showed his journal of notes. "Cows, pigs, salt, tobacco, timber and finished wood products from Shakertown, like chairs and tables, and coal and iron."

"Good research," Mom complimented. "Did you learn anything more about the history of Carrollton?"

"The settlement was established in 1792 and originally called Port William and there is a really old house still standing today named the Masterson House." Austin again referred to his journal notes. "This house is the oldest, two-story brick house on the Ohio between Pittsburgh and Cairo, Illinois."

"Here is the fact that we found the most

INTERESTING," Clayton began. "Can you believe that boats floated down the hallways of the Carroll County Courthouse during the 1937 Flood? There is a plaque on a wall in the courthouse that marks how high the water went."

"Do you think we will have time to walk inside the courthouse so we can find the plaque and take a picture?" Austin asked.

"Sounds good to me," Grampy announced.

"Oh, and something else about Carrollton," Clayton said. "Grampy, you can tie up at Point Park. That is the exact point where the Kentucky River drains into the Ohio River."

"Thanks for the information," Grampy said. "And I was thinking we could find a store that sells wakeboards."

"WAKEBOARDS?" the boys shouted.

"No kidding, Grampy?" Austin inquired as he showed that 'is he teasing us' look on his face.

"Seriously?" Clayton quizzed, as he threw his hands high in the air.

"Sure, would I try to trick you fellows?" Grampy smiled.

"Alright!" Clayton said. "Now, can I get a REAL cheeseburger for lunch?"

Chapter 11
The Runaway Houseboat

"Clayton and Austin, now that we are rolling down the river, we need to lookout for Mile Marker 535, the Vevay Towhead Sandbar, and at Mile Marker 542, the Craigs Sandbar," Grampy warned the boys. "Watch for swirling water in the Ohio, trees or tree stumps that are not flowing down the river. I have set the depth gauge warning buzzer to 10 ft. We don't want to run aground."

"Okay, Captain," Clayton said as he and Austin took their look-out post positions on the upper deck.

"Great, you guys are very helpful deckhands," Grampy said. "I have the Ohio River Navigation Chart open to that section of the river. The river map shows the possible location of the sandbars, but you never know exactly because sandbars can change due to river flooding conditions."

After about an hour of relaxing but staying alert at their posts, Austin shouted down to Grampy, "I see swirling waters on the right!"

"Thanks," Grampy answered. "Yes, I see that too. I will steer the Granny Rose to the port side to avoid the sandbar. Only 15 minutes to Carrollton! Will you fellows come down now and help Mom prepare the bumpers and ropes for tying up? This time on the starboard side. I already called the Carrollton Marina and we have permission to dock there. It is just south of Point Park."

After successfully docking the Granny Rose, the group disembarked and snapped pictures of the Kentucky River draining into the Ohio at Point Park.

"I read an article about a runaway houseboat on the Kentucky River," Mom said.

"Runaway houseboat?" Clayton inquired. "I've heard of runaway dogs and cats, but a runaway houseboat?"

"Yes, it broke its moorings from a dock in Boonesborough on the Kentucky River due to the extreme spring rains and flooding. It floated about 100 miles from there to right here over a two day period of time." Mom pointed to the converging rivers. "When it got out into the Ohio, it floated another 10 miles or so, when the Bennett

Emergency Marine Service secured it at Madison, Indiana.

"Question," Austin chimed in. "Couldn't the captain of the houseboat stop it somewhere?"

"Sorry, I didn't mention it, but no one was on board when it lost its moorings," Mom assured. "It's amazing that it floated this far because part of the dock was still attached to the boat. Maybe you can pull up something on the Ipad and find a picture of the runaway vessel."

"I found it!" Clayton cheered. "Look, there is a tree attached to the front railing, plus having the dock too."

"The article says the high water kept the boat out in the middle of the river so it didn't run into low-lying bridges or get damaged from the locks and dams on the Kentucky," Austin said. "Wow, that water had to be REALLY high for a boat to just keep traveling over the dams."

"Good thing that the owner was notified his boat was running away," Clayton mused as he picked up the cell phone and pretended to call the marine company. "Hello, Mr. Marine Emergency Service Company, could you please catch my RUNAWAY HOUSEBOAT? You will be able to recognize it out in Ohio River because it has a TREE AND PART OF A DOCK ATTACHED."

"Yes, sir, captain sir, Bennett's Service will get on it

right away!" Austin said as he and Clayton continued to laugh.

"It sounds funny now, but it could have been a dangerous situation," Mom cautioned.

"Yes, now are we ready for lunch at the Carrollton Inn?" Grampy asked.

"The Carrollton map on the Ipad shows it's about three blocks," Mom said.

"Cheeseburgers, here we come!" Clayton exclaimed, as he gave a gentle push to everyone to get moving up the sidewalk.

"Can you imagine what it would have been like to be a steamboat captain spending a day or several days at the Carrollton Inn waiting for all kinds of cargo to be transferred from small boats on the Kentucky to larger vessels on the Ohio?" Grampy asked.

"Aye, aye, Captain Grampy, our cargo is loaded and ready for the trip down the Ohio." Clayton said as he saluted Grampy. "And by the way, Austin and I checked again. We are securely tied up to the dock, so our vessel won't run away while we eat lunch."

—— Chapter 12 ——
Merging of the Rivers

Lunch at the Carrollton Inn consisted of CHEESEBURGERS WITH THE TOPS, for all the group! After walking around Carrollton, they headed back to the Carrollton Marina.

"We need to restock our food supplies," Mom suggested. "Could use some fruit, veggies, bread and sandwich meat."

"Good idea," Grampy agreed. "We will need to refuel the Granny Rose and take on some bait if you fellows want to fish this afternoon. According to our Kentucky River map, there are no more marinas until we get to Frankfort."

"Fish? Absolutely!" Austin cheered.

"Grampy, didn't you say something about WAKEBOARDS earlier today?" Clayton looked at Grampy with that joyful, eager, goofy-eyed expression on his face.

"Oh, yes, I did mention that, didn't I," Grampy grinned. "Let's see what the Marina has available."

After making their purchases, and checking the Granny Rose list for departure readiness, the group took another look at the merging of the two rivers.

"Take a look, guys," Mom pointed to the draining of the Kentucky into the Ohio. "This is the place where the Kentucky River drains from all of the Eastern Kentucky area, including the cities of Frankfort, Boonesborough, Shaker Landing, and Beattyville, where the Kentucky actually begins. The North Fork, Middle Fork, and South Fork Rivers all converge in Beattyville to form the Kentucky."

"Mom, I recall studying about Boonesborough and Shaker Village in Social Studies Class last year," Clayton said.

"Yes, and I recall learning about Harrodsburg, another pioneer settlement," Austin began, with that 'aren't you proud of me' professional look. "In the late 1700's, Captain James Harrod and Captain Thomas Bullitt brought a group of settlers down the Ohio from Pennsylvania. They traveled up the Kentucky River to Landing Run, where they followed a buffalo road to a large spring. There they built a settlement, and it became Harrodsburg."

"Right on!" Clayton gave Austin a pat on the back. "Just think – Captain Harrod and Captain Bullitt and their group were in flatboats. They had to use poles and paddles to travel on the rivers."

"And we have the 'Mansion on the River' to travel in," Austin commented. "They had no engines, electricity, sinks, kitchen, air conditioning, and on and on like we do now." Austin threw his arms open wide as if to drink in the majesty of the Granny Rose. "Thanks, again, Grampy, for taking me on this trip."

"You're welcome – again, Austin, and you know what the best thing is about this houseboat – we have showers and toilets!" Grampy nodded and smiled.

"Uh!" the boys chimed in.

"And we even have up-to-date river maps from the U.S. Army Corps of Engineers, a marine radio, and cell phones," Mom added. "Plus, we don't have to be concerned about Native American attacks. The early settlers sometimes met up with unfriendly Native Americans. They were afraid the new people were going to take over their lands and they wouldn't have the means to survive without farm land and the buffalo and other animals."

"What kind of protection did they have against

attacks?" Clayton asked.

"They used long rifles called muzzle loaders and they loaded the gunpowder into the rifle and added the lead shots," Grampy said.

"I remember a high school field trip to a re-enactment of skirmishes at Boonesborough," Mom said. "The actors used the muzzleloaders and it would take them about 15 minutes to load, shoot, and reload."

"No way!" the boys contested.

"Hey, fellows, I'm looking at my Kentucky River map and we are almost to the first lock on the Kentucky," Grampy warned. "There are three more locks to Frankfort. Clayton, here is the phone number to the first lock master. Would you like to make the radio call to obtain permission to proceed and then Austin, would you like to make the call to the next lock?"

"Cool!" the boys both agreed.

After Clayton made his first ever call on the marine radio, he sat down in the Captain's chair and wiped his forehead. "Whew! That was NERVE-WRACKING! Did I sound like a REAL boat captain?"

"Sure did," Mom expressed her approval with a handshake.

"Look," Grampy called. "Around Heath's Bend."

As the group looked to the Lock Number 1, Austin commented, "This is so different than the Markland Locks, so much smaller."

Grampy headed the Granny Rose into the lock and the lockmaster opened one gate. "This is Pool Number 1 on the river map. There is about 10 ft. difference between the Ohio River Pool and this Pool Number 1 on the Kentucky."

"Alright! It's on to Frankfort!" Clayton yelled as they completed the Lock Number 1 journey. "Grampy, can we use the wakeboards now?"

Chapter 13
Twisting, Turning and Meandering Along

"How long will we be able to ride the wakeboards?" Clayton looked at his watch.

"We have a couple of hours of twisting, turning, and meandering along on the Kentucky River until we approach the next lock," Grampy answered. "We might pass some fishermen, so you have to be careful not to disturb them. I'll be on the lookout for them and try to steer the Granny Rose away from them. We won't be passing any large towns or marinas, so this stretch of river will probably be calm with little boat traffic. You can spend as much time as you want on the boards."

"Mom, will you sit at the aft section of the boat and keep an eye out for the boys?"

"Absolutely," Mom answered. "Fellows, just give me a thumbs up sign to let me know everything is fine. Give me a thumbs down sign when you get tired or want to stop. I probably won't be able to hear you because of the noise of the engine at the rear."

"Okay! But Grampy, I..." Austin stammered. "I've never ridden on a wakeboard." He bowed his head and his face turned red.

"Hey, that's okay, don't be embarrassed, man," Clayton answered, patting Austin on the back. "Dad took me out on his friend's boat once. Wakeboarding is awesome fun"

"You can stand, kneel, lay down, or sit on the board, Austin. Then you just enjoy riding the wake created by the Granny Rose," Grampy said, retrieving the wakeboards purchased at the Carrollton Marina. He handed the boards and ropes to Austin and Clayton. You will each have your own board and ropes."

"Of course, you will be wearing your life jackets," Mom said. "You can cross over the wave, but try to stay away from the river bank. There could be tree stumps or big rocks protruding from the water."

"Ready?" Clayton waved to Austin to climb down from the mahogany swim platform into the water.

Mom waved to the boys as they positioned themselves on the boards. They gave the thumbs up sign to Mom.

"Ready in the water," Mom called to Grampy, who was at the top-side controls.

Grampy revved up the engine to create the wake from the Granny Rose and the boys stood up on the boards, laughing and smiling. They sat down, stood up, turned around, then kneeled down, splashing each other, as they gained confidence on the wakeboards.

After about an hour of riding the waves, waving to fishermen, and admiring the river environment, the boys gave the thumbs down to Mom. She pulled the ropes of the boards back to the swim platform.

"Is your skin shriveled up yet?" Mom asked the boys.

"No, not yet," Clayton laughed. "Seriously, that was major fun! We would have stayed in the water longer, but we thought you and Grampy might want a break. "Besides, we could use a snack!"

"That was totally awesome!" Austin smiled from ear to ear. "Thanks for buying us these wakeboards, Grampy."

"You're welcome," Grampy said. "Let's stop for a little while and we can all grab a snack," Grampy suggested. According to my Kentucky River map, we are at Canes

Run Creek. This is the site of a major buffalo trail that Native Americans and early pioneers followed to Big Bone Lick, the site of salt mounds. That was where the animals enjoyed having licks of salt as part of their diet. Unfortunately, some of the prehistoric large animals like the woolly mammoth and mastodon would get stuck in the marshy areas and drown. That is why it is called Big Bone Lick State Park today.

"Maybe we can visit there sometime this summer," Clayton said with expectation in his voice.

"Sure thing!" Mom answered.

After snacks, the group decided to explore the shoreline.

"Look over here!" hollered Austin. Grampy, Mom, and Clayton all ran to Austin. He was pointing to something sticking out from the bog. It was brown and white, and rounded like a bowl or pot.

"Alright, Austin!" Mom cheered. "I think you have found a Native American artifact.

Austin dug into the silt and removed the piece. "It looks like a cooking pot."

"We could take this to the Kentucky History Center along with the documents that Clayton found," Mom said.

"REALLY?" Austin smiled.

"Now, we'll both have something for the curator to see," Clayton said. "HOW COOL IS THAT?"

"Let's be on our way, break time is over. On to Frankfort." Grampy motioned to the Granny Rose.

After getting underway again on the Kentucky, Clayton asked, " I wonder why there aren't any large towns along this stretch of river?"

"I can answer that," Mom said. My friend, Rosemary Howard, has a farm in Owen County along the Kentucky River. When I stayed at her Night and Day Bed and Breakfast, I remember her telling me that back in the 1800's, there were several thriving river towns along here, like Monterey and Gratz. These towns had stores, restaurants, churches, and schools and lots of people. The population was about 5000 in Monterey, but now it's only a few hundred. The majority of people in the booming towns of years ago decided to leave the area because of the low-lying ground and constant flooding by the Kentucky in springtime. Then in the summer, the river might get so low that there would be droughts. Farmers could not make a living in these types of conditions."

"Too bad," Clayton said, shaking his head.

"Yes," Grampy agreed. "Hey, Austin, it's time for you to make the call to the lockmaster at Lock Number 2."

"Fantastic," Austin said, "I'm on it!"

"Then, when we get to Lock Number 3, Clayton, you can make that call," Grampy said.

"I will be ready and not so nervous this time," Clayton nodded.

After more twisting, turning, and meandering on the Kentucky, then traveling through Locks 2 and 3, Grampy headed the Granny Rose on to Frankfort.

"We can call our families and tell them we are staying overnight in Frankfort." Grampy handed the cell phone to Clayton and Austin. "I will call the Frankfort Boat Club and Ramp on the marine radio and ask permission to dock there. We can take on more supplies there and then fix dinner. Tomorrow morning, first thing, to the Historical Society!"

"YES!" Clayton and Austin exclaimed.

"I can't wait to hear what the curator says," Clayton added.

Chapter 14
Around the Bend to Frankfort

"We need to call Sara, the curator, and make an appointment for tomorrow morning." Grampy reached for the cell phone. "We'll also let her know we are bringing Austin's Native American artifact from Canes Creek and the Big Bone Lick area."

"This is SO COOL!" exclaimed Austin.

"Okay, we are in! Tomorrow morning at 10:00 a.m." Grampy gave handshakes to Clayton and Austin. "Sara said she is looking forward to meeting you fellows and verifying the authenticity of your treasures."

"That is seriously cool," Clayton agreed, "but look out in the river. See all that trash. That part is definitely not cool. Can we get in to see the Governor and discuss our clean up the trash campaign?"

"Don't know about that. Actually, this is our first sighting of milk jugs since we turned into the Kentucky," Mom said. "Milk jugs and other trash used to be a common sight on the Kentucky before then Governor Paul Patton proposed mandatory garbage pickup for all counties in Kentucky. That was back in 2001."

"Things have definitely improved since then, throughout the State, but, unfortunately, lots of trash still gets dumped into the rivers, like what we saw on the Ohio the other day," Grampy said. "I remember several years ago, your Granny Rose and I saw a turtle at 12 Mile Island on the Ohio River with a six-pack plastic ring around its middle. I cut the ring off and let the turtle go. He wasn't going to get any bigger the way he was growing because the shell was compressed."

"Grampy, I just looked at your river map and I see there is a bend ahead with Lock Number 4 and Frankfort coming up," Clayton said.

"Thanks, Clayton, I will call the Lockmaster right now on our marine radio, channel 13," Grampy said. "Then we will prepare to travel through the lock."

"I see the dome of the Capitol Building," Austin said excitedly as the Granny Rose rounded the bend and entered Lock Number 4.

"And I see Jim's Seafood House," Mom commented. "Excellent restaurant. We are having sandwiches this evening on the boat and finishing up the ice cream and cake from Clayton's birthday party, but let's do lunch there tomorrow."

"Received permission to tie up at the Frankfort Boat Club and Ramp on the port side, slip number 20," Grampy said. Then we will hook up with electricity, water and the sewage systems."

"We'll get the bumpers and ropes ready on the port side," Clayton said as he and Austin moved them to the left railing.

"Great, you guys are really super deckhands!" Grampy winked at the boys.

"Turkey, ham, and cheese sandwiches coming up, " Mom said.

"I'll help you, Mom," Clayton offered. "I am always ready to eat!"

After Grampy and Austin readied the Granny Rose for the night and everyone settled in for dinner, phone calls were made to families back in Louisville.

Grampy then handed the Ipad to the boys. "A good evening project for you two adventurers is to research about the history of Frankfort and any attractions we should see while we are here tomorrow, besides the History Center, of course."

"Alright! Tomorrow Austin and I get our five minutes of fame," Clayton laughed.

Chapter 15
A Sweet Surprise

"Are you ready for your fame today?" Grampy called to the boys in their lower bunks. "Breakfast is ready."

"Yes, I'm ready!" Austin said. "Hey, Clayton, wake up, man, today is our big day."

After the boys got dressed, ran up to the galley, and dived into the bacon and eggs, Clayton proudly said, "We researched last night and found out that Frankfort was settled by hunters and fur traders in the 1700's. The settlement was first called 'Frank's Ford,' and later named Frankfort, after an early settler named Stephen Frank.

"Guess what else we learned!" Austin declared. "After Kentucky became a state in 1792, Frankfort became the capital city by outbidding other cities in the state. The City of Frankfort donated land for the first capitol building, constructed in 1793. After there were four different capitol buildings, the present day capitol was constructed, beginning in 1905.

"Superb research, fellows!" Mom complimented. "We will be walking by the Old Capitol Building and the Old Governor's Mansion on our way to the History Center this morning. We will probably have time to visit those places. Maybe even take in the Kentucky Military History Museum."

"Sounds good. Time to get your walking shoes tied and grab your historic treasures," Grampy said as he pointed to the Granny Rose railing. Let's disembark immediately, like ASAP!"

"Yes, sir, aye, aye, Captain Grampy." Clayton saluted to Grampy. "Shoes tied. Documents and pottery in our hands. Ready to meet Miss Sara!"

After walking three blocks in the old historic Frankfort district, Mom said, " Look, there is the History Center Building and there standing on the steps, is a blonde lady waving to us."

"Hi, I'm Sara. You must be Clayton and Austin. Welcome to the Thomas D. Clark Center for Kentucky History. The other curators and I have been anxious to meet you and view your documents from the Ghost Ship and the pottery from the Big Bone Lick area. Follow me to the Conference Room."

Clayton and Austin could barely make their feet move, they were so excited. The group entered the rotunda of the building and heard claps from the receptionists as the boys passed the entrance desk. "Thank for bringing your findings," they heard the receptionists say.

"Please come this way," Sara said, leading the group down a long hallway to a huge room.

"Wow, look at that table," Austin whispered to Clayton. "It must be as long as a basketball court."

"Oh, yes, are you nervous? I am," Clayton admitted as he whispered back to Austin. "Who are all these people? Wait a minute! I recognize that man at the head of the table and the lady beside him." Clayton poked Austin. "Isn't that the governor and his wife?"

"Clayton and Austin, I would like to introduce you to Governor Steve Beshear and First Lady Jane Beshear," Sara said. "And these other people are our curators, who will be evaluating your findings."

"We are so happy to meet you," Governor Beshear said as he and his wife shook the boys' hands.

The boys were "quaking in their boots," but gradually relaxed as they answered the Beshears' questions about how they found the documents and the pottery piece.

The curators also asked questions. Then Sara asked, "Will you mark on these maps the locations of your findings? Plus we need your full names, addresses, and phone numbers so we know how to contact you."

Grampy and Mom helped the boys place sticky pins on the maps, and the boys signed their contact information sheets.

"We will thoroughly investigate your documents and pottery piece for their authenticity and contact you about possible placement in exhibits here at the History Center," Sara added.

At the conclusion of the meeting, Governor and First Lady Beshear approached Clayton and Austin. "Jane and I would like to present you with certificates declaring you Kentucky Colonels."

"Oh, thank you, thank you," the boys kept repeating, as Mom snapped pictures.

"AND...," the First Lady said, "we have another special surprise for you. Could you meet us at 112 E. 2nd Street at 2 o'clock this afternoon?"

"Grampy?" Clayton asked.

"Absolutely! We'll be there."

After the round of more handshakes and the goodbye greetings, Mom suggested, "Let's tour the History Center Building while we are here."

"Super." Austin agreed as he proudly said, "Clayton and I can show you the exhibits on the early Kentucky settlers, the Civil War, coal, agriculture, and a bunch more. They even have a Hall of Governors."

"Okay, let do this. Then we can get lunch at Jim's Seafood House. Of course, we are meeting the Beshears later." Grampy motioned to the entrance door of the exhibits.

"What kind of surprise do you think they will have for us?" Clayton asked Grampy.

"Don't know, but I'm sure it will be worth the wait until 2 o'clock." Grampy looked at his watch. "Only three hours to go!"

After touring the History Center and the Frankfort Historic District buildings and eating fish sandwiches at Jim's, the group began making their way to 2nd Street.

"What time is it, Grampy?" asked Austin.

"It's 1:30, plenty of time to walk to 2nd Street and find 112."

"Let's pick up the pace," Clayton motioned to the group. "We don't want to keep the Governor waiting! Can't wait until we talk to our families at home tonight. Who would have thought this adventure would lead us to the Governor. Maybe I could ask him for help with our Crosby Middle School Clean up the Trash on the River Campaign."

The group made their way over the St. Clair Bridge to 2nd Street. They saw a limo parked in front of a small white building.

"I can't read the building's sign yet," Austin said. "Do you think that is the Governor Beshear's vehicle parked there?"

Austin and Clayton ran ahead of Grampy and Mom.

"Mom, Grampy, it says Rebecca Ruth Candies!" Clayton shouted.

"Clayton, man, look up there ahead, that's Governor Beshear and the First Lady standing on the front porch of that white building," Austin said.

The chocolate aroma filled the air, as the boys greeted the Beshears. Grampy and Mom eventually caught up with the youngsters and exchanged best regards with the Beshears.

"What candy would you like? Our treat to you for being such conscientious Kentucky citizens," said the First Lady. "The candy is made right here, in this little building. You can take a tour and learn the story of the ladies who started this company back in 1919. Come on, let's go inside."

"Awesome! Thank you." The boys thanked the Beshears over and over for their hospitality.

"How are we ever going to top this adventurous day?" Clayton asked.

"Oh, there are many more twists, bends, and turns ahead of us on the Kentucky River!" Grampy answered.

"THE ADVENTURE CONTINUES!" Clayton declared.

Nautical Language

Aft
The back section of a vessel.

Bow
The front side of a vessel.

Bridge
The place in the vessel where the controls are located.
(Example – steering wheel, gears, etc.)

Captain
The first person in command of a vessel.

Channel
That part of a waterway open to navigation.

Deckhand
A helper on a vessel.

Depth gauge
A device used to measure the distance from the bottom
of a vessel to the bottom of a waterway.

First mate
The second person in command of a vessel–
takes captain's place if necessary.

Flatboat
A boat with about 2-3-ft. sides all around, no point
in front, with a flat bottom.

Moorings
Ropes and any attachments that connect a vessel to a dock.

Mouth
The point where one waterway drains into another waterway.

Port
The left side of a vessel.

Starboard
The right side of a vessel.

Stern
The rear of a vessel.

Vessel
Any sized watercraft.

Wake
Waves given off by the movement of a vessel.

Wheelhouse
The area of vessel that contains the steering controls and gauges.

Special Resources for Parents, Grandparents and Teachers

To be used with Clayton's River Adventure Continues: Cincinnati to Frankfort

Reading

Before the reading:

1) Have you ever walked on a bridge over a river?

   If yes, explain if this was a pleasant, scary, or fascinating experience.

   If not, explain what may have made it better.

2) Have you ever found anything that turned out to be quite valuable? What did you do with it?

3) Do you read comic books? Who is your favorite "super-hero?"

4) Recall a favorite experience with a friend. What made it so special?

5) Have you ever been to a restaurant from another country? Tell about any experience with unfamiliar names of food.

During the reading:

1) Why were Clayton and Austin reluctant to ask Grampy and Mom about going to the Comic Con?

2) Compare Austin's dizziness with Clayton's fear of heights. How same and different? How did the boys react to each other's problems?

3) Why did Grampy bring along his German-American Reference Book?

4) How did Mom and Grampy react to the suspension bridge, "The Shark Bridge?"

5) Why do you think Clayton, Austin, and Mom moved closer to Grampy when they heard the strange noise at the creek?

6) Evaluate Clayton and Austin's idea of calling the ghost ship, the "hero ship."

7) Was Austin nervous about riding a wakeboard? Explain.

8) Why did the once active river town of Monterey lose so many residents?

9) What law caused waterway pollution to improve in Kentucky?

10) Why do you think the Governor of Kentucky and First Lady were so fascinated with Clayton and Austin's findings?

After the reading:

1) Does this story remind you of anything you have ever experienced?

2) How were the Ohio River and Kentucky River the same and different?

Social Studies, Science, Writing, Technology

1) Using printed materials and the Internet, research about the progression of laws in your state regarding water pollution. Write letters to your state and/or local officials thanking them for efforts to clean up waterways and suggesting further laws to help the problem.

2) Using printed materials and the Internet, research about suspension bridges and present your findings on a "Science Day" at your school.

Math and Technology

1) Review Grampy's statement in Chapter 6 about the marina charges of $2.00 a foot per day. How much would it cost if the Granny Rose stayed at the dock for three days? Seven days? How much for a 24 foot vessel for one day? Five days?

2) It is about 50 miles from Carrollton, KY to Frankfort, KY. Using printed materials and the Internet, investigate the average depth of the Kentucky River at four different locations between Carrollton and Frankfort. Investigate the depth of any waterway in your area at four different locations in a 50 mile stretch. Compare the Kentucky River to the waterway in your area. Graph your findings.

3) Review Grampy's statement at the end of Chapter 7 that his houseboat needed at least three feet of water to operate. Using the information found in #2, is there anywhere that you would need to be extremely cautious so as not to run aground?

References

Belle of Louisville, Alan L. Bates,
Howell-North Books, 1965.

Chapman Piloting Seamanship and Boat Handling, Elbert
S. Maloney, 63rd Edition, The Hearst Corporation, 1999.

The Kentucky River, William E. Ellis,
The University Press of Kentucky, 2000.

Kentucky's State Capitol, David L. Buchta,
Arcadia Publishing, 2010.

Louisville, John E. Findley, Arcadia Publishing, 2009.

The Ohio River, Tim McNeese,
Chelsea House Publishers, 2004.

The Ohio River, John Ed Pearce, Photographs by
Richard Nugent, University Press of KY, 1989.

"Tourism opportunities on the rise," Owen County
News-Herald, Vol. 148, No. 20, May 20, 2015.

Visit to ComicCon, Louisville, KY, June 21, 2015.

Visit to Thomas D. Clark Center for Kentucky History,
Frankfort, KY, April 21, 2015.

Wikipedia

Interview with Jeremiah Hines, Bedford, KY,
December 21, 2014.

Interview with Rosemary Howard, Pewee Valley, KY,
March 23, 2015.

Http://www.city-data.com/city/Monterey-Kentucky.html

Http://www.expatica.om/de/about/Top-10-German-foods-with-recipes_106759.html

Http://www.frankfort.ky.gov/general-information/frankfort-history

Http://www.german.about.com/library/blmenu1.htm

Http://www.google.com/maps/place/Carroll+County+Tourism+Office

Http://www.gooverseas.com/blog/must-try-food-and-drinks-when-studying-abroad-germany

Http://www.hofbrauhausnewportky.com

Http://www.lex18.com/story/28290720/runaway-houseboat-on-kentucky-river

Http://www.newportaquarium.com

Http://www.tripadvisor.com/Attractions-g39426-Activities-c47-Frankfort_Kentucky.html

Http://www.viralforest.com/110-year-old-ghost-ship-in-the-ohio-river/

Fast Facts about the Ohio River

Runs 981 miles from Pittsburgh, Pennsylvania to Cairo, Illinois, where it flows into the Mississippi River.

In the 1500's, Native Americans apparently had a well developed civilization along the Ohio, which they called the "Beautiful River."

In the 1600's, French explorer, Sieur deLaSalle, reportedly explored the Ohio to the Falls at what is now Louisville and turned around. The next year, he explored all the way to the Gulf of Mexico.

In the 1700's, the French and English disputed over the river territory, and the English eventually drove the French out. A trading post for the early settlers was opened in Pittsburgh.

In 1778, George Rogers Clark led a group of settlers from Pittsburgh downriver to Louisville at the Falls. Riverboats could not navigate the 25 ft. drop in the water level.

In the 1800's, the Portland Canal was built around the Falls of the Ohio to allow riverboat traffic to continue beyond Louisville, providing better access to the Midwest at St. Louis and to the South at New Orleans.

In the 1900's, a system of locks and dams was built on the Ohio providing even easier access for riverboat traffic.

From the 1800's to today, the U.S. Army Corps of Engineers oversees the Ohio River.

Today, the Ohio River is home to approximately 120 species of fish, and a decreasing population of wildlife along the river.

About the Author
Linda M. Penn

Linda M. Penn holds a master's degree and Rank I degree in Elementary Education from the University of Louisville. She taught kindergarten through third grade for twenty-one years in public schools.

Linda's first book, *"Is Kentucky in the Sky?"* won the Silver Medallion from Mom's Choice Awards. Her second book, *"Hunter and the Fast Car Trophy Race"* features a young boy who loves stock car racing. *"Clayton's Birding Adventure,"* her third book, features a youngster who moves to a new neighborhood and school and makes friends in an unusual way. *"No More French Fries in the Bed,"* Linda's book with the returning characters of Allyson and Samantha was released in 2015.

"Clayton's River Adventure," written with Linda's cousin, Frank Feger, brings Clayton and Austin back, this time returning in an adventure on the Ohio River.

Linda's website and blog, **lindampenn.com** contains many resources geared for parents and teachers to enhance the reading experience with their young ones. You can read her blog about writing and reading for children and download the educational resources for free. To contact Linda, you can email her at lindampenn@gmail.com.

About the Author
Frank Joseph Feger

Frank was born in Louisville Ky., and graduated from St. Xavier High School and United Electronics Institute with a degree in Electronics. As a Vietnam era Veteran, he served three years in the U.S. Army.

Frank was a Medical Electronics Sale Representative for 40 years. He worked for Malkin Instrument Co. and sold pacemakers, defibrillators and cardiac monitors for 10 years. He worked for Olympus Medical Corp. for 30 years and sold gastrointestinal endoscopes in Kentucky, Indiana and Ohio. Frank retired in 2007 and is the VP of the Colon Cancer Prevention Project in Louisville, Ky.

Feger has been a boater for 55 years. The boat mentioned in the book, *The Granny Rose*, was a 42-foot Harbor Master Houseboat that made two trips to Cincinnati. Frank and his family enjoyed the boat and the trips all his family and friends embarked on.

At a family reunion, Linda and Frank met upon an interesting boating conversation. Linda had already been thinking about publishing another Clayton book, and upon hearing Frank's river traveling stories, the two decided to mesh their experiences together and embark on another Clayton adventure–this time down the Ohio River.

About the Illustrator
Matt C. Adams

Illustrator Matt C. Adams resides in northern Kentucky with his fiancé, Suzanne, their four children, Justice, Gabe, Reed and Avery, and their faithful hound, Jessie. Matt has previously drawn editorial cartoons for the Oldham Era, a local newspaper, illustrated Clayton's River Adventure, and seen his artwork printed in IDW Publishing's Transformers Spotlight: Grimlock (2009). He hopes that you've enjoyed his artistic take on Clayton and the rest of the *Granny Rose* crew and their adventures on the Ohio and Kentucky Rivers. As always, please join Matt, Linda and Frank for more Clayton Adventures in the future.